UNREPORTED MIRACLES

What You Probably Do Not Know About Your Child's School Bus

Dr. Cal LeMon

The Executive Edge

KENDALL/HUNT PUBLISHING COMPANY
4050 Westmark Drive   Dubuque, Iowa 52002

Back cover photo by Rock-A-Fellow.

Copyright © 1998 by Cal LeMon

ISBN 0-7872-4893-2

All rights reserved. No part of this publication may be reproduced, stored in a retrieval system, or transmitted, in any form or by any means, electronic, mechanical, photocopying, recording, or otherwise, without the prior written permission of the copyright owner.

Printed in the United States of America

10 9 8 7 6 5 4 3 2 1

CONTENTS

Introduction v
Acknowledgments ix
Your Bus Quotient xi

CHAPTER ONE **SAFETY IN NUMBERS** 1

CHAPTER TWO **THIS YELLOW ALWAYS RUNS** 9

CHAPTER THREE **THE DANGER ZONE** 21

CHAPTER FOUR **THE THREE POINTS OF SEATBELTS** 31

CHAPTER FIVE **WHO IS IN THE DRIVER'S SEAT?** 41

CHAPTER SIX **THE NEXT STOP** 47

Buswork 57

INTRODUCTION

Monument Building

I am a father, husband, corporate trainer, professional speaker, fly-fisherman, incurable pack-rat, Michael Bolton wannabe and, until three years ago, did not give a rip about yellow school buses.

Maybe you are like me. These bright, yellow wheeled-whales would sometimes yuk up my commute to and from the office with their staccato stops, flashing lights and interminable waits for little, pencil legs to jump off that last metal step. I did not hate . . . or love these yellow, bouncing buckets of bolts touting their finger-painted messages to me on fogged windows.

While providing a keynote address in San Diego for the California Association of School Transportation Officials (CASTO), my attitude toward school buses permanently changed. As a matter of fact, I had a conversion experience!

A group of leaders from CASTO asked to have breakfast with me the day following my address. This was the second time I had spoken for this group and they immediately started the bagels around the table with congratulations on both the content and delivery of my address. I was appreciative; but clients normally do not take me to breakfast to hand out bouquets.

Once the sausage and eggs were history, we got down to the purpose of our meeting. I quickly found out that the safety of children in California was being compromised because money for buses was being redirected to other "pressing" educational needs.

I was interested but not convinced. I asked for specifics. Two school districts in California had actually eliminated bus transportation for children (which was reversed when outraged parents demanded reinstatement for elementary children); walking distances had been extended to five miles in some communities; unregulated "van services" were becoming the new California growth industry; and unattended six and seven year olds were boarding public transit buses.

The clink and clank of china cups sliding into indented saucers was the only noise for a while. Then I asked, "What does this have to do with me?"

These new friends asked if I would design and implement a public awareness program throughout California about the safe and smart choice to put our children on yellow school buses.

I promised I would think about the offer because, at that time, I did not need another professional "challenge." There would have to be a compelling reason, beside making more money, to become a crusader for a vehicle which, in my opinion, just made my commute longer. School buses are just there, but they are not a cause!

Then I had a birthday. I inched up to the big 50. Both of my kids were in college or graduate school icing careers with great grades and stellar recommendations. My thirty year marriage was content and comfortable (we were well past the "who left up the lid?" and "I used to make you laugh" stages). And my business was doing so well I could not find time on my calendar to get a haircut. But, I still needed to build a monument!

It is my personal opinion that once you get through mid-life crisis, the next stage of life is what I call "monument-building." This is the time when scooping up money and momentos pales in contrast to leaving something intangible which will scream, "Cal LeMon was here."

So I'm writing this book and investing myself in school transportation for a very selfish reason—this is one of my monuments. I have been building monuments through my kids, my church and my friendships; but, I wanted to build something more than just a company. Safely transporting children to and from school sounds like a great way to use up a life.

We give flapping lip service as to how "our children are our future" and they are "our best natural resource;" but all of that is so much sloppy sentimentality unless we ensure their physical safety.

I, like you, want to find meaning in my work. Part of my work is to inform you that yellow school buses are the safest and smartest form of ground transportation for our children. When we make other choices, we compromise our verbal commitment to our children.

So, for the past three years I have immersed myself in the specifics of "compartmentalization," the requirements for CDL-qualified drivers, "fuel-tank integrity" and an encyclopedia of "bus things" (as my kids call it).

Who, among my friends and family, would have believed this subject could be one of the passions of my later life? Well, yellow school buses have actually taken me for a ride. The ride has been to a place where I can . . . build a monument.

Please read this book for what it is: a call to make a safe and smart choice for the safety of your children. Is there a better legacy for any of us?

ACKNOWLEDGMENTS

Writing a book is the hardest work I do. The transformation of thoughts into words has, alternately, exhilarated and exhausted me. This endeavor, I can assure you, is not a one-man-show.

So, it is with genuine thanksgiving that I thank and celebrate the following people and organizations.

To the members of the CASTO Public Awareness Committee: Don Fowler, Doug Snyder, Larry Laxson, and Verna Borders—thank you for teaching me how to "bleed yellow."

To the manufacturers and contractors: AmTran Corporation, A-Z Bus Sales, Blue Bird Bus Corporation, California Bus Sales, Laidlaw Transit, Navistar International Transportation Corporation, Ricon Corporation, Santa Barbara Transportation, and Thomas Built Buses—thank you teaching me that safety is your business.

To Karen and Robin—thank you for so gracefully dealing with the bytes, bits and bloopers of my office.

To Charlie Gauthier, Executive Director, National Association of State Directors of Pupil Transportation Services—thank you for keeping me honest with your incredible willingness to edit this work.

To Bill Paul, Editor, *School Transportation News*—thank you for promoting school bus public awareness with your press and personal passion.

And to the school bus drivers and pupil transportation officials I have met across the U.S. and Canada—thank you for giving parents everywhere the incredible safety record to refer to your work as, **unreported miracles.**

YOUR BUS QUOTIENT

Before reading this book, take the following quiz to determine your knowledge of school bus issues. Circle **true** or **false** for each item. The answers, along with the page numbers where you will find additional information, are on the following page.

1. School bus transportation infrastructure is the largest system of ground transportation in the United States.

    True   **False**

2. There is approximately 75% of all K-12 students in the U.S. who daily ride yellow school buses to and from school.

    True   **False**

3. Over 200,000 public school buses are on the roads each school day in the United States.

    True   **False**

4. Most crash-test research suggests the two-point seat belt is safer than the present school bus seat design called "compartmentalization."

    True   **False**

5. There are more than 100 Federal, state, provincial, and local government agencies and industry associations involved with school transportation in the United States and Canada.

    True   **False**

xi

6. Bus driver candidates are mandated by the federal government to submit to drug testing and criminal background checks.

        True   **False**

7. Funding for school transportation usually takes 10% of every dollar allocated for education.

        True   **False**

8. The U.S. Department of Transportation requires school buses manufactured after April 1, 1977 to be equipped with a metal cage designed to protect the fuel tank in a direct 30 mph collision by a two-ton vehicle.

        True   **False**

9. The passenger car is statistically a much safer vehicle to transport children in than the yellow school bus.

        True   **False**

10. The National Safety Council calls the school bus the safest form of ground transportation in the United States.

        True   **False**

Answers to the Bus Quotient Quiz

1. True (Please see page 4)

2. False (Please see page 4)

3. False (Please see page 4)

4. False (Please see page 35)

5. True (Please see page 11)

6. False (Please see page 41)

7. False (Please see page 48)

8. True (Please see page 19)

9. False (Please see page 2)

10. True (Please see page 2)

Chapter One

Safety in Numbers

We live our lives "by the numbers." Think about it. The numbers ticking by on your wrist rule your day. The numbers in your checkbook jerk around your moods. And the number of candles on your last birthday cake can flash an unbelievable total as you scan your "going south" body or massage a creaking knee.

Numbers also determine our willingness to risk. We take chances based on numbers. For a cool $1.00 you can have a 1 in 3 million chance of becoming a millionaire in most state lotteries. Not great odds, but who cares for $1.00? What if the lottery ticket cost $1,000.00? Would those numbers (the odds of your winning) make any difference?

But risking money is not the subject of this book; bodies are the issue here. Dr. Abraham Maslow reminded us that physical "safety" is the second strongest primitive motivation in humanity's "hierarchy of needs." In other words, no one has the time or energy to debate the national debt, write a sonnet or clean out a junk drawer if he or she is not physically safe.

Consider the personal safety we practice every day by picking up a banana peel, buckling a seat belt, locking a door, wearing ear muffs when it is cold, putting on SP40 when it is hot and repeatedly looking over a shoulder in a strange neighborhood.

So some of us have looked at the numbers and have decided that even though 34 people died downhill skiing last year, those digits do not keep boots from crunching into bindings. Even though 800 fun-seekers lost their lives teetering on a two-wheeler, a run around the block would still be fun. And even though drunk drivers killed approximately 19,000 of us last year, millions will "take their chances" after sipping a potent brew.

But this book is not about faceless statistics. These pages are honed around the flesh and blood you know best: your children. Since you are responsible for the care, nurturance and safety of your child, numbers, when they scream physical harm, do get your attention.

Therefore, try these numbers. You probably will not hear them on the evening news or see them in headlines.

According to the National Safety Council in 1996, here is a comparative chart showing the risk of death to a passenger in the following transportation modes. This study was conducted in the United States in 1994 on the transportation death rate per 100 million passenger miles traveled.

CHART 1.1	
Passenger automobiles	0.86 (a school bus is 172 times safer)
Railroad passenger trains	0.04 (a school bus is 8 times safer)
Scheduled airlines	0.04 (a school bus is 8 times safer)
Transit buses	0.02 (a school bus is 4 times safer)
Intercity buses	0.02 (a school bus is 4 times safer)
School buses	Less than 0.005

1996, National Safety Council

As you can see, the "numbers" broadcast a strong message:

Your child's school bus is the safest form of transportation in this nation.

I did not know these numbers. As a parent I was always demanding that my kids wear their coats, wash their hands and never kiss guys who even look like they could be a carrier for some gross disease. But I never thought about the ways they were getting to and from school and school-related activities. Whether it was shoving their warm little bodies into my car or somebody else's, it really did not matter. But it does.

As a matter of fact, it is a matter of life and death.

To illustrate, join me in the back of a large hotel ballroom after I made a presentation to a national pupil transportation conference.

As I was gathering my overhead transparencies and greeting people, I saw a woman waiting to speak to me. I moved toward her and she extended her hand while I watched her eyes fill with tears. She said, "My son would be alive today if he had heard your message."

It was the end of the school day at Davis County High School in Owensboro, Kentucky. There was an electric excitement in the air because it was December 8, 1995 and, not only was it close to Christmas vacation, it was snowing! The flakes, big as dollar pancakes, started to quietly sit on each other. The Kentucky pine trees were getting dressed for winter and the kids were ecstatic.

Charles Nicholas Brown, like his classmates, was darting out the door for home. Charles had a special reason to get home as soon as possible—his two horses needed to be fed and cared for before the weather turned really bad. The weather man kept droning on about a possible accumulation of six inches to a foot.

One of Charles' friends offered to take him home. The yellow school buses had snaked their way into position and Charles was suddenly seized with a decision. His mother, Clara, was a driver. Charles knew what she would say. This sixteen-year old young man decided in favor of the fastest route to his horses.

His friend lost control and the Browns lost a son. Clara, with tears cascading, said to me at the back of that hotel ballroom, "The safest trip home for Charles would have been that school bus."

Every morning over 400,000 yellow school buses ply the farm roads, streets and super highways of this country. Nearly 25 million students get on and off these buses each school day. These buses travel 4.3 billion miles annually. These numbers equate to 100 million boardings and deboardings daily, or 18 billion boardings and deboardings during the typical nine month school year. This does not count the trips and boardings and deboardings related to school activities.

Now, let us go back to the first chart in this chapter. Using 100 million passenger miles as the "common denominator" for each of the transportation modes, your child has a less than 0.005 chance of loosing his or her life when riding a yellow school bus.

Those zeros followed by the five are obscene digits to any parent who has lost a child. All of us want that number to read, 0.000. Any death or injury is already in the "unacceptable" column. But, life is a chance; there are no guarantees.

It seems to me all parents would want to play the best odds for their children. If I told you, prior to you placing your child on a scheduled airline flight, there was a 25% chance the flight would tragically end...you, undoubtedly, would take your child and exit the terminal. Those odds are unacceptable.

Well, I have a question. Why would only 54% of all K-12 students in the U.S. be riding a yellow school bus in the morning when the numbers scream this is the safest trip our kids will take any given day? I understand there are many children who walk to neighborhood schools. But what about the millions who are piling into private cars driven by inexperienced drivers, riding in unregulated van shuttle services or boarding unsupervised public transit vehicles?

Am I suggesting parents no longer drive their children to school or make the final choice on a mode of transportation? No. I am suggesting there are numbers, statistical evidence, every parent should know before making those decisions.

Until three years ago, I did not know the numbers. Driving my kids to school was just another "no-brainer" in my daily schedule. The only numbers I ever knew about school buses were how many kids were injured or killed in a particular school bus accident when it occurred. Those stories always made the front page.

There is no press for a school bus which safely makes its regular stops and provides **millions** of boardings and deboardings each day. But the video cameras whine and the reporter's lips lap at microphones when a yellow bus is hit by a tractor semi-trailer or ends up in a ditch.

You know what: that is news. It is important news that in October of 1995 a commuter train traveling approximately 60 MPH collided with the rear end of a stopped school bus in Fox River Grove, Illinois leaving seven students dead and 24 injured. It is important news that on December 6, 1995 in Los Angeles a malfunctioning trash truck raked the side of a school bus with protruding metal arms and killed two children.

News is made when "something out of the ordinary" takes place. Not too many newspapers will send a reporter and photographer to cover the regular, ho-hum boarding of a passenger railroad car. It is when that steel cylinder is upside down in a creekbed that the news machine comes alive.

The following composite numbers for fatalities in school bus transportation are news. You have a right, and obligation, to look at them closely. They should make the front page in all of our minds.

As you can see, from 1986 through 1996, an average of 13 occupants of school buses (including school bus drivers and passengers) were killed each year in crashes. That is 13 too many.

CHART 1.2
Fatalities In School Bus-Related Crashes 1986–96

	Occupants of School Bus*			Pedestrians			Other Non-	Occupants of	
Year	Driver	Passenger	Total	Struck by School Bus*	Struck by Other Vehicle	Total	Occupants	Other Vehicle	Total
1986	2	0	2	31	16	47	6	73	128
1987	8	9	17	32	11	43	5	113	178
1988	2	6	8	19	17	36	6	80	130
1989	4	33	37	25	7	32	1	72	142
1990	4	7	11	32	7	39	1	64	115
1991	2	15	17	21	5	26	5	86	134
1992	1	9	10	21	8	29	2	83	124
1993	1	12	13	32	8	40	2	86	141
1994	2	2	4	28	9	37	2	64	107
1995	0	13	13	24	10	34	4	72	123
1996	2	8	10	16	7	23	2	101	136
TOTAL	28	114	142	281	105	386	36	894	1,458
Avg.	3	10	13	26	10	35	3	81	133

*Includes school bus body type and vehicle used as school bus.
Source: National Highway Safety Traffic Administration, Traffic Safety Facts, 1997.

But contrast that number with 25 million students who were transported to and from school each classroom day and, I believe, you will also hear the beginnings of **"unreported miracles."** Is it not miraculous that all those children could be moved from their homes to school and back again with this safety record?

While I am passing out the noisemakers and throwing the confetti for the big yellow machine party, we probably also need to wake up and smell another set of numbers.

Parents, educators and citizens have some significant challenges in education as we enter the next millennium. Student populations are and will be exploding.

School enrollments will increase 33 percent between 1990 and 2030. This will add 4 million additional children by 2005 and 15 million by 2030. The next chart will illustrate the reason why you may believe your child's school is becoming "crowded."

Dubbed the "baby boom echo," additional children are flooding our classrooms, hallways and school buses. While educators are strategizing on how to raise national test scores, keep the best teachers and maintain safe, comfortable classrooms, there is another issue...transportation.

As school budgets get smaller and classroom rosters get larger, pupil transportation often has to take a backseat (sorry!). The squeeze for bucks sometimes results in concrete thinking which goes something like this, "Well, it seems to me the issue is books or buses." Books is the hands-down winner.

Unfortunately, our children lose this argument. The books vs. the buses mentality totally misses a larger issue: children cannot move to the top of Dr. Maslow's hierarchy to experience "self-actualization" if they are not physically safe.

Equally, if we get children to the classroom safely but have sacrificed the integrity of the learning, nothing has been gained. Parents should remind all parties involved in their children's education that **interests,** not **positions** is the goal. The finger-wagging and posturing over "books or buses" is the position but does not

8   Unreported Miracles

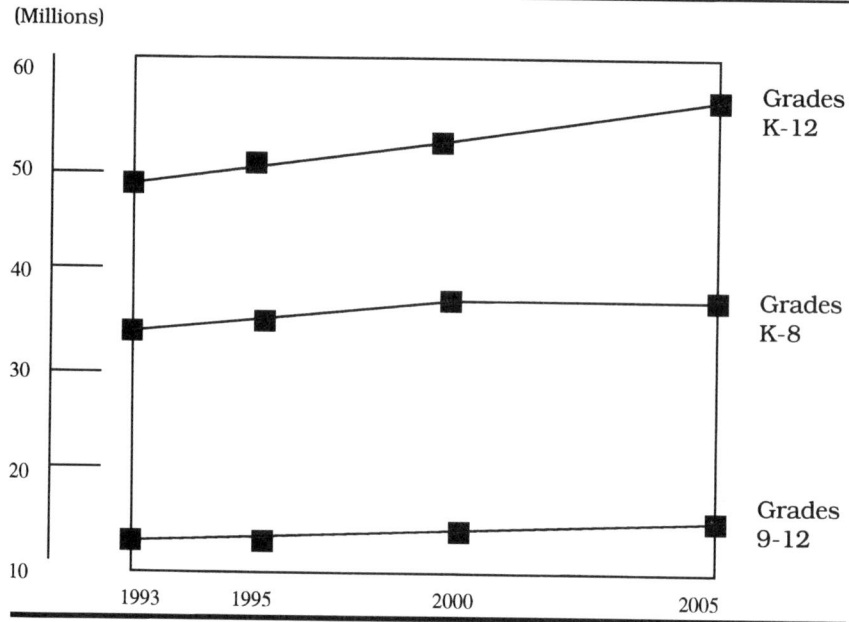

Source: National Center For Education Statistics

address the interest. Everyone's interest, from the superintendent to the bus driver, is to offer excellence in education. That shared interest will always guarantee our children will win.

It is in the interest of excellence in education that I remind all of us, **the front door of your child's school should be painted yellow.** We simply cannot argue with the numbers. The statistics, as you have seen in this first chapter, are amazing...even miraculous. To move 25 million children twice each day with minimal risk is the miracle which will not be covered on the 6 p.m. news.

Chapter Two

This Yellow Always Runs

The number, 0.005, is no accident. This statistical "chance" your child has of loosing his or her life as a passenger on a yellow school bus is the result of the federal and state government, education leaders, industry engineers and people, like yourself, diligently working together to ensure safety to and from school.

Trace, with me, how we got to this miraculous number, 0.005.

When the first settlers stumbled over the cold, gray rocks of the Massachusetts shoreline, they brought with them a commitment to the education of their children. Between the pew and a parent's knee, children learned lessons in faith and family.

By the late 1800's education had been institutionalized in the "school house" where the community provided a teacher and a pot-bellied stove. As the country expanded, so did the distances children were traveling to get to the classroom. The predecessor to the school bus was often a horse-drawn wagon with a teenage "driver" who would follow a familiar route picking up children along the way to a consolidated school.

By 1910 thirty states had pupil transportation programs in place. Part of the "right" of education in the United States was also the guarantee of a ride to school. But with the expansion of the nation's highway systems in the 1920's and 1930's, the country was finding a "ride" was not enough; it had to be a safe ride.

I have discovered that the safety features built into your child's bus have often been designed out of tragedy. As this nation sprinted into world leadership, it flexed its political and industrial muscles on endless miles of concrete. In 1910 there were almost 0.25 million miles of all-weather, hard-surfaced roads in the United States. By the end of World War II paved roads had sky-rocketed to 1.5 million miles. No sooner had a new road been built and it was gurgitating fumes and...accidents. The promise of a better life, a life on wheels, was literally killing us and our children.

When school bus accidents snuffed out the emerging flicker of new lives, our emotional rip-cord was pulled. Something had to be done.

In 1939, representatives from 48 states gathered to declare reason and sound design were the only answers to reversing the horrific death and injury statistics. This group called for national "standards" which would guarantee a safe ride on any school bus regardless of location in the country.

The standards developed at this conference in New York City were divided into two parts: chassis standards and body standards. The 17 recommendations for chassis standards covered items such as axles, batteries, brakes, bumpers, gasoline tanks, tires, and weight distribution. There were 27 recommendations for body standards which addressed aisle widths, ceiling heights, door specifications, lights, mirrors, seat spacing, etc.

The only problem with these standards is they were not legally binding. In other words, if a school wanted to put a bus on the road which did not meet these standards, a call from a lawyer would do no good. An unsafe bus was not a violation of any law.

In 1966, the Congress stepped in, after reviewing the alarming statistics which showed the carnage from motor vehicle crashes on the nation's highways, by passing two significant pieces of legislation. The Highway Safety Act of 1966 was directed at the development of Highway Safety Programs that states could implement to reduce accidents and resulting injuries and fatalities. One of those programs dealt specifically with the operational issues surrounding pupil transportation, such as school bus driver training.

The National Traffic and Motor Vehicle Safety Act of 1966 required the establishment of Federal motor vehicle safety standards to ensure that any motor vehicle was designed and manufactured in such a manner that its performance would protect the public from "unreasonable risk of accidents, injuries, and fatalities." Through both of these Acts, the Congress established a "baseline of safety requirements for all motor vehicles, including school buses."

The agency responsible for reviewing, writing and enforcing these standards is the National Highway Traffic Safety Administration (NHTSA), an agency of the U.S. Department of Transportation. The responsibility of the manufacturer is to certify the buses coming off their assembly lines are in compliance with these standards.

As a result of the passage of the National Traffic and Motor Vehicle Safety Act, and follow-up legislation called the School Bus Safety Amendments of 1974, NHTSA has issued 33 Federal motor vehicle safety standards that apply to school buses. These standards are divided into two groups: (1) crash avoidance—vehicle features that will help avert a crash; and (2) crashworthiness—features that will help reduce injuries and fatalities if a crash occurs. This second category also includes post-crash requirements—features to help reduce injuries and fatalites resulting from fuel leaks and fires. The list on page 12 will give you an overview of the items on your child's school bus which have minimum requirements established by NHTSA.

While a number of these Federal motor vehicle safety standards have special requirements for school buses, five of them should be of special interest to all parents:

1. School bus rollover protection

2. School bus body joint strength

CHART 2.1
Federal Motor Vehicle Safety Standards that Apply to School Buses

No.	Standard
Crash Avoidance	
101	Control Location, Identification and Illumination
102	Transmission Shift Lever Sequence, Starter Interlocks and Transmission Braking Effect
103	Windshield Defrosting and Defogging Systems
104	Windshield Wiping and Washing Systems
105	Hydraulic Brake Systems
106	Brake Hoses
107	Reflecting Surfaces
108	Lamps, Reflective Devices and Associated Equipment
111	Rearview Mirrors
112	Headlamp Concealment Devices
113	Hood Latches
115	Vehicle Identification Numbers
116	Motor Vehicle Brake Fluids
119	New Pneumatic Tires
120	Tire Selection and Rims
121	Air Brake Systems
124	Accelerator Control System
Crashworthiness	
Crash	
201	Occupant Protection in Interior Impact (a)
203	Impact Protection for the Driver from the Steering Control Systems (a)
204	Steering Control Rearward Displacement (a)
205	Glazing Materials
207	Seating Systems (Driver's Seat)
208	Occupant Crash Protection (Driver)
209	Seat Belt Assemblies (b)
210	Seat Belt Assembly Anchorages (b)
212	Windshield Mounting (a)
217	Bus Window Retention and Release
219	Windshield Zone Intrusion (a)
220	School Bus Rollover Protection
221	School Bus Body Joint Strength (c)
222	School Bus Passenger Seating and Crash Protection
Post crash	
301	Fuel System Integrity
302	Flammability of Interior Materials

(a) Applies only to school buses with GVWRs of 10,000 lb or less.
(b) FMVSS 209 and 210 apply to driver's seats on all school buses and to passenger seats on school buses with GVWRs of 10,000 lb. or less.
(c) Applies only to school buses with GVWRs greater than 10,000 lb.

This Yellow Always Runs   13

3. School bus passenger seating and crash protection

4. School bus pedestrian safety devices

5. School bus fuel system integrity

In the next few pages, I will walk you through these standards to reinforce that "unreported miracles" take place every day because your child's safety is the foremost concern of federal and state government and manufacturers.

To ensure the structural integrity of a school bus in the event it is involved in a rollover crash, the manufacturer uses steel trusses in a design called "roof bows." The standard stipulates that the roof must be able to withstand the pressure of one and a half times its unloaded weight.

In other words, if the unloaded weight of a bus is 30,000 pounds, that bus roof must be able to endure the pressure of 45,000 pounds of force.

In the Fox River Grove, Illinois school bus accident when the commuter train hit the rear end of the bus at approximately 60 MPH, eye witnesses said the impact was strong enough that "the body of the bus separated from the chassis." In this instance, the separation of the body from the chassis was an asset to the occupants.

Inspite of its tragic consequences, this accident could have been even more deadly if it were not for the body strength standard. The bus did not tear apart on impact. If the riveted joints on the side of the bus had been torn apart, the loss of life would have been greater.

Well, how strong does that joint have to be on your child's bus? Let me put it this way. If I put a piece of aluminum in a mechanical device which would tear it apart by pulling from each end, it may require 20,000 pounds of pulling power. If I try the same with a piece of steel it may require 50,000 pounds of force. Each joint on a school bus (where two pieces of metal are joined together) must be able to endure 60% of the pulling power of the **weakest** mate-

Rollover Protection

Courtesy of BM&A: Blackwood/Martin & Associates, Inc.

Body Joint Strength

Photo courtesy of Rock-A-Fellow.

rial. In other words, if there is a joint made with one side aluminum and the other side steel, it would be 60% of the 20,000 pounds of force for the aluminum (the weakest substance) or 12,000 pounds of pulling power.

Hello, are you still with me? You know what the bottom line is: your child's school bus is subjected to intense joint testing. This standard is unique to just school buses.

The Federal Motor Vehicle Safety Standards mandate a seating arrangement and construction called, "compartmentalization."

16 Unreported Miracles

Passenger Seating and Crash Protection

Photo courtesy of Rock-A-Fellow.

The purpose of this standard is to wrap your child in a protective environment when the bus is involved in an accident.

This standard simply mandates that the seats must have high backs, be well-padded, have strong anchorages to the floor, be evenly-spaced, and face forward, thereby creating, what I call, "a safety cocoon," for your child.

The distinct advantage of compartmentalization for your child is—it is a passive system. That means your child does not have to do something to activate the safety feature. Compartmentalization is always there to protect your child in the event of a crash.

Chapter Four will give further details about this seat standard when we look at the issue of seat belts on school buses.

The next standard requires school buses to be equipped with an automatic stop signal arm on the left side of the bus to help alert motorists that they should stop their vehicles because children are boarding or leaving a stopped school bus.

Pedestrian Safety Devices

Photo courtesy of Rock-A-Fellow.

There is no crash which caused greater concern about school bus safety than the 1988 news accounts of a Kentucky church bus which was hit head-on by a pickup truck headed the wrong way

18 Unreported Miracles

Fuel System Integrity

Photo courtesy of Navistar International.

on an interstate highway. The driver of the truck was legally drunk.

In the ensuing collision the bus caught on fire and 24 children and 3 adults lost their lives. Yes, this was a church bus, but it was purchased by the First Assembly of God Church in Radcliff, Kentucky from a school.

The fuel tank was obviously the focus of attention by NHTSA in the aftermath of that crash.

As school bus standards have been improved over the years, the Department of Transportation has mandated that all buses built after April 1, 1977 come equipped with a metal cage built around the fuel tank so it will not leak after a direct 30 mph impact by a two-ton vehicle. The Kentucky bus chassis came off the production line on March 23, 1977—nine days before the federal law took effect. When the bus was built, the protective cage was just an option, not a requirement.

There is a very sound process in place to ensure that motor vehicles, including school buses, comply with all applicable Federal motor vehicle safety standards. NHTSA establishes a standard and advises manufacturers how to test their vehicles for compliance with those standards. Manufacturers have the responsibility to conduct sufficient engineering analyses and testing to "certify" that when their vehicles come off the assembly line that they meet the applicable standards.

As part of its enforcement activities, NHTSA periodically purchases new school buses and conducts tests to see if the vehicles actually "measure up" to the Federal standards. If NHTSA determines that a vehicle or group of vehicles does not comply with a standard, then those vehicles must be recalled by the manufacturer and be brought into compliance with the standard, at no expense to the owner. In the next chapter we will see an illustration of this practice with your child's school bus.

The message is clear with all of these standards, the newer your child's bus is, the greater the safety factor.

The good news of this chapter is while you are reading these words there are legislators, engineers, manufacturers and transportation officials who are constantly making the statement, "We can do better." There is a goal here—the numbers should read 0.000 chance of a fatality on a school bus.

Chapter Three

The Danger Zone

In the book, *Into Thin Air,* John Krachaur catalogues the fatality-strewn ascent of Mt. Everest in 1996. The reader soon learns that anyone who climbed above 20,000 feet had entered the "death zone."

At this altitude, the climber's tissues and cells can no longer recreate themselves. Fat can no longer be stored. The body begins to call for fat deposited in muscles in order to move. Thoughts and movements become sluggish. It is in this zone that many seeking the summit have just sat down in sub-freezing temperatures and never stood up again.

Pretty scary place.

Well, using the same analogy, there is a "danger zone" around your child's school bus which must be understood and responded to with rational parental action. The worst choice is to do nothing. This is an area of your child's safety over which you can take some control. For the past 25 years there has been exhaustive data collected which paints the same picture:

your child is safer inside than outside a school bus.

Using the fatality statistics (Chart 3.1) from the school years 1986 through 1996, what is your conclusion?

With the exception of 1989 when an horrific crash took the lives of 21 students, the largest number of fatalities take place outside the school bus. As a matter of fact, a pedestrian is three times more likely to lose his/her life than an occupant.

Using the fatality statistics from 1992 through 1995 (Chart 3.2) as a representative sample, watch the specifics of your child's danger zone come into clear view.

When kids are going home after six to eight hours of sitting at the same desk, cruising the same halls and trying to add up the same mind-numbing column of numbers, it's party time! The school bus becomes a kid "happy hour" on wheels. This short person is probably winding down for a relaxed night of video games, telephone gossip or MTV.

CHART 3.1

Year	Occupant Fatalities	Pedestrian Fatalities	Total Student Fatalities
1986	0	47	47
1987	9	43	52
1988	6	36	42
1989	33	32	65
1990	7	39	46
1991	15	26	41
1992	9	29	38
1993	12	40	52
1994	2	37	39
1995	13	34	47
1996	8	23	31
Average	10	35	45

Source: NHTSA

CHART 3.2
School Children Killed

	1992	1993	1994	1995
Going to school	6	6	12	11
Activity trip	0	0	0	0
Going home	14	22	7	14
No information	2	4	1	0
Total	**22**	**32**	**20**	**25**

Do you remember the feeling? Anyone out there recall singing this little ditty on the last day of school?

> "No more pencils, no more books
> No more teacher's dirty looks."

The exuberance of "getting out of here" often clouds judgment. Our children forget some of the rules just like we do when we are extremely angry, extremely happy, extremely rushed, extremely . . . anything. They often do not look both ways or stay in the line of sight of the driver. In the last 25 years of record keeping, the trip home has always logged the greatest number of accidents.

There is another issue. When children are leaving a bus, the driver has been trained to make sure that students are safely away from the bus before he/she pulls back into traffic. Human error has, obviously, taken place in some of these accidents. As precise and complete as the machinery has become, there is still the chance for the driver to "miss" seeing something important.

Since 1991, there have been seven incidents where a child was killed because a drawstring from some new trend in "baggy" clothing or a drawstring on a backpack got caught when the child was exiting the bus. All of these drawstrings had a large bobble or knot at the end.

After learning of two incidents involving students being killed when their drawstrings were caught on school bus handrails, NHTSA opened safety defect investigations into the handrail designs of every school bus manufacturer. Although the safety problem was the result of changes in clothing designs, the school bus manufacturers voluntarily recalled several hundred thousand school buses to change handrail designs that had been safely in use for decades.

There are several things you can do to eliminate this danger zone:

1. Talk to your child(ren) about the importance of observing good safety practices, especially at the end of the day. Discuss how those wonderful feelings of having worked hard can create lapses in judgment which can be fatal.

2. Instruct your child to *never* go back to pick up a piece of paper, book or any other item which may be lying near the bus upon disembarking. If the driver has watched your child move out of the danger zone, his/her attention is back to moving the bus into traffic.

3. Closely look over your child's clothing and backpacks—if you find any drawstrings, **CUT THEM OFF!** At least shorten them so they cannot get caught on anything.

There is some other important information you need to know about drawstrings on your child's clothing. There have been almost twice as many fatalities when drawstrings have been caught in playground equipment and fences on school property than on any part of a school bus.

CHART 3.3
School Children Killed by School Bus

Child's position when killed	1992	1993	1994	1995
Front of bus	9	14	6	9
Back of bus	2	9	5	3
Total	**11**	**23**	**11**	**12**

The front of your child's bus (Chart 3.3) continues to be another danger zone. The obvious issue is the driver cannot see your child for one major reason—children are short and the driver may not be able to see them when they are too close to the front of the school bus. If the driver begins to pull away from the school bus stop, and a child is in front of the bus, but not within the school bus driver's direct vision, a serious danger exists.

There are several devices which have dramatically narrowed this danger zone. The first is a series of mirrors mandated as one of the Federal 33 standards for school buses. These mirrors make it possible for the driver to check the "blind spot" directly in front of the hood and on either side of the bus.

Photo courtesy of Rock-A-Fellow.

26   Unreported Miracles

The second device is called a "crossing gate" which immediately is deployed when the bus door is opened. In the next picture you can see how this barrier keeps the front of the bus off limits to a child eager to get home after a hard day of playdough and multiplication tables.

There is another safety feature which is not on the bus, but is the bus. Among manufacturers there are four "types" of buses. For our purposes I want to explain the "Type C" and "Type D." On the next two pages you will see the difference.

As you can see, the Type C bus or the "conventional" design has a protruding hood. The Type D or "transit" design gives the

Photo courtesy of Rock-A-Fellow.

Type "C": Navistar chassis and Thomas body conventional school bus. Photo courtesy of Thomas Built Buses.

driver a "look down" position which provides an unobstructed view of all areas except the first several feet in front of the school bus. From 1992 to 1995, Type C buses had 11 pedestrian fatalities and Type D had 5. Those numbers do not make Type C buses unsafe; they do show that the better visibility from a Type D bus can be an asset to safety.

This danger zone can be minimized if you will:

1. Instruct your children to always make sure he/she can see the bus driver's face when crossing in front of the bus.

2. If you have small children, go to the bus stop and walk off, with your child, at least ten feet on the exiting side of the bus, then, with the driver's approval, have your child walk in front of the bus.

3. Support the best safety device on your child's school bus— the driver.

28   Unreported Miracles

Type "D": Thomas Saf-T-liner® ER rear engine school coach. 84 passenger. Sides and front above windshield have Reflexite® reflective tape. Photo courtesy of Thomas Built Buses.

Accidents in the "danger zone" are usually attributable to human error. Since we all have "feet of clay" we can understand a mistake. But mistakes can be minimized with training, training and more training. School bus drivers need excellent equipment but they also need continuous updating of their skills. Your support of more training for the driver of your child's school bus is the best way to bring down the injury and fatality statistics.

CHART 3.4				
School Children Killed by Vehicle Passing School Bus				
	1992	**1993**	**1994**	**1995**
Passing vehicle	6	6	6	10
Other	5	0	3	3
No information	0	3	0	0
Total children killed (school bus and other vehicle)	22	32	20	25

The last part of the danger zone does not have anything to do with your children, a bus manufacturer, a design flaw or the driver. It has to do with adults, people like you and me, who see the red lights blinking and the stop arm extended from the side of the bus but decide they "don't have the time" to stop.

The numbers do not lie. Almost 40% of all the fatalities in and around the loading and unloading of school buses are directly related to the public's attitude toward a stopped bus. (Chart 3.4)

There simply is no excuse. The "passing vehicle" category in this chart can and should be eliminated. We do not, as a society, condone the abuse or neglect of children. How could we tolerate such flagrant violation of our values! There are some areas of life which must be roped off as sacred. A stopped school bus with the red lights flashing should be one of those areas.

If you want to know if drivers who pass a stopped school bus is a problem in your community:

1. Contact your child's bus driver to get a first-hand appraisal of the number of cars which illegally pass a stopped school bus.

2. Use the resources of the following national associations whose purpose is to provide your child with the safest ride possible.

National Association for Pupil Transportation
120 Washington Avenue, #100
Albany, New York
1-800-989-NAPT

National Association of State Directors of Pupil Transportation Services
1604 Longfellow Street
McLean, Virginia 22101
703-734-1620

National School Transportation Association
P.O. Box 2639
Springfield, Virginia 22152
703-644-0700

3. Write down the license plate number of a violating vehicle and immediately report it to the police.

4. If you feel strongly about this issue, write as a guest columnist in your local newspaper's editorial page a plea for adult participation in the safety of your children. This is a powerful medium.

What is the cost, in dollars, of the danger zone? Based on sophisticated mathematical formulas, federal officials have concluded that the lifetime cost of each life lost in a crash in the U.S. is $803,000.00. Included in this total are medical expenses, property damage, lost income, etc. This means the 25 children killed in the loading and unloading zone of a school bus in the 1995-96 school year will cost $20,075,000. Add these dollars to the emotional cost and the conclusion is clear: all of us need to do more to reduce the fatalities and injuries when children get on and off a school bus.

The "Danger Zone" is real. It's parameters have been historically etched in tragedy. The worst choice, like the ill-fated climbers of Everest in 1996, is to sit down and lose the initiative to move forward. Students can be spared injury and death through increased education, design of new equipment and parents who vehemently defend the right of their children to be safe.

Chapter Four
The Three Points of Seatbelts

I kept procrastinating writing this chapter. After a little conversation with myself (I believe there are some healthy benefits to talking to yourself), I realized it was internal resistance to dealing with this issue.

Every time I make a public presentation on the subject of school bus safety there is the inevitable question, "Why don't school buses have seat belts?" There is a well-founded answer, but I'm not sure my audiences can always hear it.

There is an initial distinction I need to make. In this chapter when the term "seat belt" is used it will mean a lap belt with just two anchoring points. A "safety belt," on the other hand, is a three-point system which includes a shoulder harness.

Let me begin by reminding you there is no one in the government, manufacturers or pupil transportation services who would intentionally ignore a potential safety hazard. Please remember, most of these people are parents too. The quick response by the Federal government and the school transportation industry to the drawstring danger, the fuel tank cage, the stop arm, the specialized mirror requirements, and hundreds of other improvements all clearly say: the business of pupil transportation is safety.

And safety, believe it or not, is the reason there are not seat belts on school buses.

The argument for seat belts at first glance, seem to make sense:

1. "If safety belts are so important in cars and vans, how can we eliminate them on school buses?"

2. "We give our children double messages when they have to buckle up in a car but not on a school bus."

3. "Seat belts would guarantee safety in a bus rollover."

4. "Seat belts would restore order on school buses."

5. "Fatalities and injuries would be lowered or eliminated if every child were secured in a seat belt."

You know what, those may be good reasons to put seat belts on buses. But "good" reasons are not always smart reasons.

All parties in this debate must first agree to an important ground rule: a final solution cannot be forged on the spongy surface of sentiment. The safety of our children must be decided by parents and experts who have examined the data. If we make decisions because we watched a video of a crashed school bus at 6 p.m. or heard NBC's *ER*, Dr. Doug Ross, say after examining incoming patients from a school bus crash, "When are they going to put safety belts on school buses?", we are victimized by a society which measures truth in Nielsen ratings. Our children deserve smart decisions made on the basis of fact, not feelings.

Before we closely examine the facts behind the National Highway Transportation and Safety Administration (NHTSA) recommendation that seat belts not be placed on school buses, there is an important point to make.

You will find seat belts on some school buses. NHTSA does require seat belts on buses with a gross vehicle weight rating of under 10,000 pounds. These are the smaller school buses with a seating capacity which usually does not exceed 20 occupants.

Seat belts are required in these small school buses since their size, weight, and construction are similar to that of the family car, light truck, or van. Such features affect the crashworthiness of a vehicle, and the need for passenger restraints to provide occupant crash protection.

NHSTA has not required seat belts for school buses over 10,000 pounds gross vehicle weight (GVW). There are two states, New York and New Jersey, which have, on their own initiative, required seat belts on these larger buses.

So you will find seat belts on small school buses and in states where they have been mandated by the state laws.

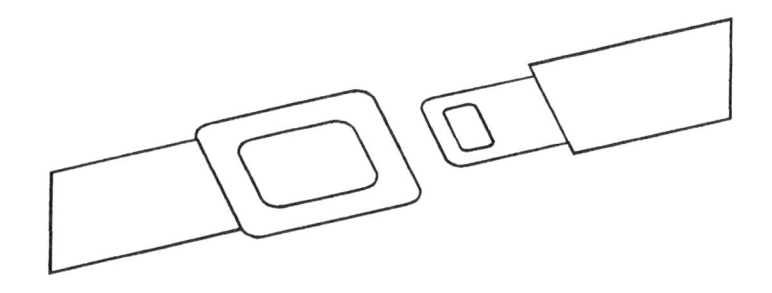

First, seat belts are not required on school buses because a large school bus is not a car. That is not patronizing double-talk.

We assume if police are giving tickets for not wearing your automobile seat belt and every parking lot exit posts a sign, "Buckle Up," the rules should be the same for yellow school buses.

Contrast these vehicles. Most automobiles place the passenger's feet approximately 18 inches off the road surface; the head is normally within 30 inches of the windshield in the front seats; there are numerous protrusions on the dashboard; the frame is intended to support the "look" or is non-existent above the occupant (convertibles); and many automobiles augment the use of a safety belt with an air bag system.

The design of a bus body places the passenger's feet approximately 30 inches above the road surface which protects the occupant from direct side impact crashes. This is the main reason over-the-road motor coaches, transit buses and school buses are not required to have either seat belts or safety belts for passengers.

For the passenger, there are no dashboard protrusions on a school bus. Your child slips into a seat which comprises a passive safety system. The system is called "compartmentalization."

Second, seat belts are not required on school buses because compartmentalization has proven to be a passive, effective form of school bus passenger restraint.

The Federal School Bus Passenger Seating and Crash Protection standard requires strong, well-padded, evenly-spaced, forward-facing, energy-absorbing seating which does not require your child to do anything to be safe. In the event of a crash, the system provides for impact against the energy-absorbing seat in front of the occupant or the padded side panel. As a caring parent, you want to know, "Does this system really work?".

Since we agreed this discussion would be built on data, not emotion, we need to look at the testing results to decide if compartmentalization is better or worse than mandating seat belts.

If you are like me, when I need to know the right answer, I will consult an "expert." If the question has to do with my body, I will call my physician. If I am in doubt about a decision which has legal implications for my business, I will call my attorney. I have to trust the people in my life who invest their careers in one specific area. Let's do the same here.

The last time there was statistical evidence gathered on this issue, it was the late 1980's.

In 1987, the National Transportation Safety Board completed a detailed analysis of 43 serious accidents involving large school buses. The Board reached several conclusions concerning seat belts, most notable that most school bus occupant fatalities and serious injuries were "attributable to the occupants' seating position being in direct line with the crash forces. It is unlikely that the availability of any type of restraint would have improved their injury outcome."

In other words, if a 30,000 pound school bus is directly hit by a 75,000 pound tractor semi-trailer, seat belts or safety belts would not be a factor in survivability for those occupants directly in line of the crash.

The NTSB, the experts in crash evaluations, concluded after investigating these 43 serious accidents that: (1) in most of the accidents seat belts would not have made any difference in injury outcome, (2) in a few cases, seat belts would have reduced injuries and fatalities and, (3) in some cases, seat belts would actually have caused fatalities or increased injury levels. The bottomline to this long, and detailed study:

The National Transportation Safety Board found there is no net positive benefit to seat belts on school buses and that school buses with compartmentalization provide extremely safe transportation to students without the need for seat belts.

Please note that the NTSB investigated the aforementioned Fox River Grove, Illinois railroad crossing crash which took the lives of seven and injured 24 of the occupants. Their conclusion, after exhaustive testing and examination of the crash site, was seat belts would have undoubtedly raised the fatality count. The students in the back of the bus only had milliseconds to react to the oncoming train to move quickly to the front of the bus. Unlatching seat belts would have taken additional milliseconds which would have cost more lives.

In 1989, the National Academy of Sciences completed a study at the direction of the United States Congress on "the principal causes of fatalities and injuries to school children riding in school buses and of the use of seat belts in school buses and other measures that may improve the safety of school bus transportation."

The Academy was directed to "determine those safety measures that are most effective in protecting the safety of school children while boarding, leaving, and riding in school buses." In its conclusions, the Academy noted that "the overall potential benefits of requiring safety belts on large school buses are insufficient to justify a Federal requirement for mandatory installation."

To back up that conclusion, here are some numbers for your consideration. During 1995, 12 occupants in a school-bus-body type vehicle died in a crash. While each of these fatalities was a tragedy that everyone wishes had never happened, those 12 deaths pale when compared to the 8,168 children between the ages of 5 and 20 who died as passengers or drivers in all other types of motor vehicles during the same year.

We learned in Chapter Three that the real danger zone for your child is *outside*, not inside a school bus. Serious accidents are so rare for large school buses that a study on seat belt effectiveness in New Jersey, one of the states which has mandated their installation and use, has been delayed because there is not sufficient data for statistical comparisons.

If the danger zone is outside the bus, would it not be better to turn attention to ideas like loudspeakers for drivers to warn children and the public of deboardings, electronic or mechanical sensors to detect children within 10 feet of the school bus body or improved cross-view mirrors?

The findings of the NTSB and NAS confirm compartmentalization has definite advantages as a passive restraint system for your child's safety.

In addition, there are other dangers with lap belts, especially to smaller children, which need to be explored.

When you strap yourself or your child into a seat belt in your car or van, you will use a "three-point restraint" system. Do you remember when only lap belts were required in automobiles? In 1968 all of that changed when the effectiveness of the "shoulder" harness was proven to dramatically reduce fatalities and injuries.

Lap belts, when used in school buses built after April 1, 1977 (compartmentalization was mandated), have two serious flaws as an active restraint system.

First, with younger children (3 through 12 years of age) there is the danger of "submarining" (sliding out of the lap belt when the school bus is involved in a rear-end collision) and sustaining significant internal injuries.

Physiology is at the center of this debate. As an adult you can feel the top of your hip joints (anterior superior iliac spines) which are approximately an inch above your thighs. This bone structure encases your pelvic area. When you put on a lap belt across this area, the belt is supported on either side by this skeletal structure.

This is not the case with small children. The iliac spines or hip joints are still developing until about age nine or ten. The child does not begin to form secondary ossification centers in this skel-

Photo courtesy of Rock-A-Fellow.

etal area until about the age of 12 in girls and ages 13 or 14 in boys. So in younger children there is cartilage which is still flexible and conforming to external trauma.

In a decelerating crash (the school bus comes to a sudden stop), the rigid seat belt will not meet the resistance of a skeletal frame and will drive the belt into the internal organs. This trauma can cause extensive internal bleeding, crushed kidneys, ruptured bladders and spinal injuries.

There is a second physiological reason why the lap belt may be injurious. In 1985, the Council on Road Trauma of Hamilton, Ontario, Canada, conducted scientific crash tests on three school buses with anthropomorphic dummies. Using video cameras and body sensors, the buses were driven at 30 mph directly into a concrete wall.

The conclusion from Transport Canada was, "The use of lap seat belts in any of the 3 sizes of recent model school buses which were tested may result in more severe head and neck injuries for a belted occupant than for an unbelted one, in a severe frontal collision."

What is going on here that this test would come up with that conclusion? When the child was restrained only in the pelvic area, the head was thrust into the back of the next seat creating extreme pressure on the neck and spine. In the words of the study, ". . . restrained dummies were generally subjected to higher maximum resultant head accelerations, more sudden head accelerations, and more severe extensions of the neck than unrestrained dummies."

As you can see, the data suggests there are some significant concerns about using just a lap belt with the passive compartmentalization system.

Well, what about the 3-point "safety belt" as an alternative? This is one of those situations where we cannot have it both ways.

It is an engineering possibility to put safety belts on school buses. The anchoring of the shoulder harness would, of necessity, make the seatback more rigid in order to endure the energy of a crash. In effect, compartmentalization would not be necessary, or advisable, because of some of its energy-absorbing qualities.

I think you see the problem. The school bus has to have either a three-point safety belt system or compartmentalization. The safety belt will work well if **everyone** is buckled up. If 10 percent of the students in a 60 passenger school bus are unbelted in a severe crash, they become victims of an interior that is not as "occupant-friendly" as compartmentalization. The advantages of compartmentalization have been sacrificed for the goal of having 100% compliance that everyone will "buckle up."

There is a question bouncing around in my mind right now, "Is 100% compliance realistic?" The latest compliance statistics from the National Safety Council on passenger car usage of safety belts is approximately 60 percent. Even in New Jersey, from my personal conversations with pupil transportation professionals, a significant number of students do not use seat belts even though there is a mandatory seat belt policy in school buses.

Let's put all of this together on why compartmentalization is the best choice:

1. The experts have concluded, after the best scientific research, there is no identified safety problem in large school buses that the installation of seat belts would solve.

2. There are strong physiological arguments against using seat belts, especially with smaller children.

3. The three-point safety belt is an effective restraint system but would require the elimination of some critical components of compartmentalization.

Third, seat belts are not required on school buses because monitoring this active restraint system would decrease the driver's ability to safely operate the bus.

Some of the larger school buses have an approved seating capacity of 84 passengers. Consider for a moment, all of the children enter the bus and take their places and now the driver must come down the aisle and visually check to make sure each occupant has his or her seat belt attached and is wearing it correctly, low around the hip bone.

What happens to the driver's concentration when the seat belt is released while the bus is moving? What happens to a driver's concentration when an unused seat belt hits a child in a sudden stop? What happens when the seat belt is used as a weapon by another child? What happens, and this is a horrendous thought, if the bus is on fire or in a major accident and the driver is hurt and cannot assist a child to release a seat belt?

One of the options, and several school districts have used this, is to hire "bus monitors" who would make sure seat belts were used and used correctly. There is a financial cost to consider here. Back in 1977 the Southwest Research Institute conducted a research project in California entitled, "Study Relating to Seat Belts for Use in Buses." The conclusion was (in 1977 dollars) it would cost $45,670,000 per year to place monitors on large buses in just this one state. Can you imagine that cost today!

This chapter has provided three, information-based reasons why seat belts are not required by the Federal government on larger school buses. I am asking you to carefully consider the facts and reasoning here.

While the seat belt debate will most likely continue, we need to keep asking, out loud, is this the best use of our attention and resources? Are there other areas of your child's school transportation that actually need more immediate attention?

The stakes are high here. We are making decisions for the people who matter most to us...our children. We cannot afford to offer their futures up on the altar of adult argumentation.

Chapter Five

Who Is in the Driver's Seat?

This yellow-encased collection of rivets, rims and roof-bows is only as safe as the throbbing, flesh-and-blood human being who daily dents the driver's seat. You have learned that the design and construction of the yellow school bus is without parallel in the transportation industry. But there is an unknown here: who really is the person with your child, literally, in his/her hands?

Let's start with what every school bus driver in the U.S. must know and be able to do before opening those glass doors at the first stop.

As recently as just 12 years ago, there were no Federal regulations with respect to the licensing requirements for school bus drivers. In 1986, Congress passed the Commercial Motor Vehicle Safety Act which required all states to significantly modify their existing licensing, testing and background requirements for all commercial drivers which included school bus drivers. For anyone who wants to drive a large school bus (one that seats more than 16 passengers), he/she must possess a valid Commercial Driver License (CDL). Today there are over 512,000 CDL-qualified school bus drivers in the U.S.

States are free to move beyond this minimum requirement by adding their own, unique training programs. As a matter of

Photo courtesy of Thomas Built Buses.

fact, most states now require a valid CDL to drive any size school bus.

To illustrate how states have "raised the bar" on perspective school bus drivers, look at what is required of someone in California who wants a yellow career. You will notice, no one walks in off the street one day and starts driving your children around the next in California.

California state law requires each school bus driver applicant to successfully complete a minimum of 40 hours of instruction. This detailed instruction offers 20 hours spent in a classroom with a state-certified instructor and 20 hours behind-the-wheel with the same instructor sitting right beside the would-be school bus driver. From personal conversations I have had with people who have gone through this program, "intense" would be a good adjective to describe their learning experience.

Drug and alcohol testing, criminal background checks and an extensive first-aid training program are all additional requirements, beyond the CDL and 40 hours of instruction, for the new California school bus driver.

California is not alone. Arkansas recently required The National Safety Council's "Defensive Driving Course for School Bus Drivers" program for all school bus drivers in the state. In Delaware, all drivers must be able to successfully operate an emergency radio network or other communication device. The Indiana House of Representatives has required criminal history checks for any employee whose duties involve direct contact with children.

It is not uncommon in some state school bus training programs for applicants to be taught how to respond in a hijacking situation, how to discipline unruly students, how to physically handle a convulsing child, how to fill out an accident report, how to emotionally respond to an irate parent and how to teach riders what to do in the event of an emergency.

Think of the complexity of skills required to drive a school bus. On a larger bus it is possible to have 84 children behind the driver! How do you cope with two or three kids in your car or van who are screaming for no apparent reason, putting bubble-gum in someone's hair or "flicking" (index finger propelled from tension with the thumb) a seat-mate's ear? On family vacations, I could handle the noise and whining until I heard slapping skin. Then it was time for my tried and proven, "Do you want me to stop this car?" number.

Can you imagine having up to 84 children in the vehicle you are responsible for safely driving and then getting them to their correct stop without accident and injury? There is the traffic to watch, the correct signals to activate, dashboard gauges to check, a glance in the mirror to monitor behavior, stairwells to observe, exterior mirrors to check (sometimes two and three times), the "danger zone" to observe, the cars behind you and the oncoming traffic. All of those acts probably took place in less than one minute.

What does someone get paid for being a skilled professional entrusted with the safety of your children?

In 1977, Florida's Wakulla County, starting pay was $7.22 per hour and in Fairbury, Nebraska bus drivers averaged $10.00 per hour. The national average is about $11.00 per hour with limited benefits. Contrast those numbers against public transit drivers who make up to $20.00 per hour plus full benefits.

The reason I am raising this issue of compensation is to alert you to a growing problem in pupil transportation. Tougher licensing requirements, low national unemployment statistics, more difficult behavioral issues to handle on a school bus and non-competitive wages have created a serious shortage of school bus drivers. With public school enrollments going up and calls for greater safety standards also escalating, this problem will only get worse.

With all of the requirements and low-pay, why does someone decide to be a school bus driver? After speaking to and with drivers for the past three years, I have come to the following conclusions:

1. Many school bus drivers initially accepted this responsibility because the "part-time" quality of the job met their immediate lifestyle needs. They may have been completing a degree, raising a family or needed to supplement another income source. This is the reason why there is still such a significant turn-over in this profession.

2. Then there is the "bleeding yellow" group. These are drivers who have decided to make a career in pupil transportation and just enjoy physically handling these large machines while interacting with the kids. They are personally committed to their work and know just about everything in this profession. They are so dedicated they now "bleed yellow."

3. The final group not only bleeds yellow but are, what I call, the "second-milers." These school bus drivers can maintain discipline, never have an accident, know their yellow machine inside out, and bring a very special desire to go that second mile for your children. A "second-miler" in my opinion may be Nancy Kent or Karen Arnzen.

For 18 years, driving a school bus was always much more than a job for Nancy Kent at the Delaware Valley Central School District on the Pennsylvania/New York border. Nancy believed her job description, even though it did not appear in some driver's manual, required her to always go the second mile. The second mile mentality saved the life of one of her riders on January 19, 1996.

No where in her training was Nancy required to wait until children turned the knob on the front door before she pressed her foot to the accelerator. When it was hunting season, or there was severe weather or an unfamiliar car was parked nearby, Nancy would patiently wait until the child entered his or her home.

On this cold, January day, Nancy waited at her last stop while 13 year old Disaree Fox and her sister, Tamara, walked across a small footbridge on their path from the school bus to the front door. Nancy was concerned that the footbridge was still intact after recent heavy rains.

The sisters went across the footbridge with no trouble, then continued up a road with water rushing down one side. Suddenly, Disaree appeared, from the bus, to "fall down," but she did not get up. What both sisters had not realized was the road had washed out and filled with water which had a thin coating of ice on it. Disaree had fallen through the ice and started to scream for help.

As Tamara started running to the school bus, Nancy grabbed a tire chain and ran to Disaree. Pulling the teenager to safety, Nancy hustled both of them back to the bus where she put the heater fan on high and wrapped the shaking child in her coat.

If driving this bus had been a "job," Nancy Kent should have pulled away when those children were 10 feet away from the bus.

If she had "gone by the book," Disaree may have become another statistic.

With 84 handprints of children stitched on a quilt wrapped around her shoulders, Karen Arnzen of Knumclaw, South Dakota savored the delights of going the "second-mile."

The hands were traced by the K-6 children Karen drove to school last year. This "friendship quilt" was one of six stitched by bus drivers in a team-building project for drivers and those children they regularly transport to school.

Karen Arnzen said, "Driving a bus is a lot more than getting kids from point A to point B. You have to care about kids, especially when you're turning your back on them. A bus driver becomes a confidant, a counselor . . . a kid just wants an adult to listen to them for a few minutes, and that's all it takes."

Consider this for a minute: your child's first contact with the educational process every classroom day begins with the school bus driver. Not only does this person know what RPM is needed to shift to a higher gear but the majority of these professionals also know when to ask, "Is everything all right?". The "second-milers" are wonderfully talented and caring people who would, and have, given their lives for the children who sit behind them.

Are there careless, uncaring, inappropriate school bus drivers? To answer "no" would fly in the face of reason. There are over a half a million people who drive school buses and the laws of average would dictate some should probably not be behind the wheel.

But what percentage fall into that category? It has to be minuscule. The first reason the percentage has to be infinitesimally small is not too many unqualified applicants will be willing to go through the stringent evaluation and training program. But the second reason I know the driver of your child's bus is a competent person is, **the unreported miracles**. Billions of safe boardings and deboardings take place every year, not just because there is a mechanical arm which flipped out from the bumper or four red lights over the emergency back door which started blinking, but because the person operating that machine **cared** about the cargo.

CHAPTER SIX

The Next Stop

Notice the title of this final chapter is not, "The Last Stop." When it comes to the safety of our children, there is no finality, there is no "perfection." As long as there are statistics to examine, there will be work for all of us to do.

The purpose of this chapter is to highlight some important issues which will affect the quality and longevity of yellow school bus transportation as we know it. If you believe, as I do, that school buses are one of the things that "work" in America, you will be interested in these next few pages.

There is a crisis developing in the school bus industry and it is funding. Yes, bucks and buses do go together. We can debate, for the next millennium, good intentions for the safe transport of our children to and from school, but "good intentions" are cheap words unless we put our money where our hearts are.

During 1996, an average of $493 per child was spent to transport regular education children and $2,461 per child for students with disabilities. The requirements that schools provide transportation to students with disabilities is based on the Rehabilitation Act of 1973, the Individuals with Disabilities Education Act of 1990 (formerly the Education of the Handicapped Act), and the Americans with Disabilities Act of 1990.

The bottom line is this:

on average, approximately 4% of the yearly cost of educating your child is spent on pupil transportation.

The per child cost of regular education runs anywhere from $4,000.00 to $9,000.00 per year depending on the state. Many state governments fund only 50% of the total education bill. Local school districts must find additional tax moneys, from the community coffers, to keep the school doors open.

Your child's school bus is squarely in the cross-hairs of the education funding dilemma in the United States. When local school boards have to increase teacher's salaries to keep the best in the classroom, maintain buildings which are warm and dry, constantly build new classrooms for the burgeoning X Generation's xettes, supply books which do not have 50's illustrations, buy computers to prepare our children for the 21st Century—where do you think school buses fall among these priorities, especially in states where school transportation is not mandated?

Yellow is beginning to disappear across the landscape of this county. In some communities, pupil transportation services are being severely curtailed or eliminated. Since I have been working with the California school bus community, I have some first-hand information. Look at the following list:

> Fremont Union High School District
> Saratoga Union Elementary School District
> Los Gatos Union Elementary School District
> Los Gatos-Saratoga Joint Union High School District
> Romoland Elementary School District
> Union Elementary School District

All of these school districts have either reduced or eliminated student transportation because, when it came to a choice of buses or books, the books won.

When yellow school buses cease to cruise the streets of any community there usually are three choices for most parents: (1) Lengthen the walking distances (in California there are some communities where the legal walking distance is seven miles before a child can qualify to be picked up by a school bus), (2) Put the kids in the car or hire a van service to take them to school, or (3) Place children on public transit.

If the safety of your child is the reason you are turning these pages, all three of these options should concern you.

We learned in the first chapter the statistics scream it is 172 times safer to usher your child up that school bus stairwell than pile them into your vehicle. Again, I am not suggesting you should never drive your child to school. I am suggesting there are data which prove the yellow school bus is a safer choice.

And what about the two million children every school day who climb on to a public transit bus to go to classes? Transit buses are a well-maintained, safe and reliable form of transportation. That is not the issue here. The issue is, where are the calls for seat belts on these machines which have an interior studded with metal bars and plastic seats? Why do the children who ride public transit buses not need the protection of stop arms, compartmentalization or flashing red lights?

Now, here's the rub. We have come full-circle because we are back to the funding issue. Transit buses receive Federal moneys to subsidize the fare box. In my community of approximately 200,000 citizens, the Federal government kicked in three million dollars last year to keep the city buses on the street. Unfortunately, school buses do not have the same access to this funding source.

If you, as a parent, insist on safe transportation of your child to and from school, and you believe this safe ride is an integral part of the educational process, then it will cost us. The tragic irony of this situation is, as parental demands for safety increase without adequate funding, the exact opposite occurs — safety is compromised. If school boards cannot afford to keep buses on the road, then our children are the ones who ultimately lose. All of the statistics confirm the yellow school bus is your safest and smartest choice for school transportation, but if we refuse to fund our best intentions, then the buses are parked and we spin the roulette wheel on our children's safety.

This brings us to the second major concern for the future of pupil transportation: the use of the "non-conforming" van.

Several years ago eight-year-old Jacob Stebler, along with his classmates, were on a school field trip in Columbia, South Carolina when the van in which they were riding was struck broadside by a large truck. Jacob was killed.

There are two specific problems with non-conforming vans (generally carrying twelve to fifteen passengers). First, these vehicles are not manufactured to the same stringent Federal motor vehicle safety standards as the yellow school bus. For example, vans are not as large and heavy as a school bus, and are not built with the same rollover protection, body joint strength or passenger protection of compartmentalization. Vans just do not offer your child the same built-in, passive safety features of a yellow school bus.

Second, these vans, when exclusively used for school services such as running regular routes and activity or athletic trips, have been purchased in violation of a Federal law. That law prohibits dealers from selling or leasing such a vehicle to a school unless it meets the Federal school bus safety standards. Ford Motor Company, General Motors Corporation, and Chrysler Corporation must provide notification to each of its dealers of the Federal law as a reminder not to sell/lease passenger vans with seating capacities of more than 10 persons to schools.

Unfortunately, most states do not have laws making it illegal to purchase and use such vehicles for transporting our children. As a result, many school districts, private schools, entrepreneurs are still using vans for home-to-school transportation and a host of "activity trips."

Federal law defines a "bus" as any vehicle which can carry more than 10 passengers. Fifteen passenger vans are being altered by taking out seats or placing a large wooden box over some seats in order to get the seating capacity under the 10 passenger limit. If it is not a "bus," some enterprising business person would say, then Federal requirements do not apply. This is a mistaken assumption.

Think carefully about placing your child on one of these "kiddie cab" vans. There are over 250 van companies in the United States which skitter around communities daily picking up children. These companies have flourished when walking distances have been stretched or school bus transportation curtailed or ended.

Many of these van companies diligently work at being safe. They have installed additional mirrors, equipped each occupant with a three-point safety belt and printed "School Bus" in bright lettering. But the fact still remains, a van is not a school bus.

There is another important issue: the driver of the van is not required to have a CDL (commercial driver license) and a specialized school bus driver's license as required by most states. The background check, drug and alcohol testing, first-aid training and behind-the-wheel instruction may not be part of this person's preparation to move your child safely around your streets.

It seems to me the same passion which has been brought to the seat belt issue should be applied to transporting children in nonconforming vehicles. Can we really afford to pick and choose a "cause" when our kid's lives are on the line?

The third issue you may begin to hear about is advertising on school buses. In the interest of generating additional income (Minnesota is presently funding a major part of the Head Start program through voluntary school bus advertising on a district by district basis), some states and local school districts have permitted advertising on the exterior of school buses.

There are three important issues which surround a school bus visually hawking a product or service. Those issues are the content, legal challenges to the content and, most important, the potential safety consequences. For the purposes of this book, let's look at the safety concerns.

School buses are painted yellow for a reason: they are easy to see. When that patch of yellow begins to loom on the surface of the road in front of you, your mind immediately registers the purpose of this vehicle. The majority of the public will begin to slow down, and motorists will watch carefully for any foot traffic around a stopped bus and then exercise caution until the yellow disappears.

Think about it for a minute, the purpose of advertising is to catch your attention. Have you ever found yourself reading a message or trying to figure out a non-verbal sign on the side of a truck, transit bus or taxi cab? As a matter of fact, it is the non-verbal ones which often captivate me. I am still laughing over the transit bus sign I saw in a large midwestern city which had a man holding a comb over an almost bald head (my personal issue) with every strand standing straight on end. The words cascading over this traveling ad for a cellular phone company intoned, "We won't give you any static." Cute.

If that message was draped across the side of a school bus and children were milling around this 15 ton machine, would I still have the same concentration on how my actions may affect the safety of these children? As a business owner, I do not advertise my services unless I am assured the message will get the attention of potential clients.

The problem with this argument against or for advertising on school buses is the issue is so new we do not have data to determine which side is statistically correct. I would rather not move our children around like pawns on the chessboard of our highways to prove a point. The record of yellow school buses is excellent. Why would we tamper with what we know is already saving lives and avoiding injury?

You will notice the three pending issues I have raised for you to consider (reduction or elimination of pupil transportation, non-conforming vans and school bus advertising) all have been launched as a result of a lack of funding. If money were not an issue, I would like to now drive you into the future and show you the possibilities for an even safer trip to school for your child.

On the next page you will find a "concept bus" designed and built by the Blue Bird Corporation. If it looks strange, you are right! This is not the same bus that picked me up for school in Atco, New Jersey 43 years ago.

Ultra safe ultra low emission natural gas school bus. Photo courtesy of Blue Bird corporation.

This bus, like many others on the drawing boards of major manufacturers, is designed around safety.

We begin with the driver. Data Vision, a heads-up display developed by Delco, conveniently projects all the instrument readings, route information and warning messages right onto the front windshield. Obviously, this feature allows the driver to keep his/her eyes trained on the road ahead.

The driver also has a series of video cameras which provide real-time visual contact with the sides and rear of the bus. When the door is opened, the windshield display projects a clear picture of the side of the bus provided by this video camera. Likewise, when the bus is put in the reverse gear, the heads-up display shows what is directly behind the bus.

This school bus also includes emergency locking lap and shoulder safety belts integrated into the upper seat padding. There is an on-board learning center complete with a VCR, video monitors and speaker system so a child's learning can begin before ever entering the school building.

High intensity discharge lighting (HID) was used for all the doors, exterior safety, and low beam headlight functions. The daytime running lights come on automatically with ignition and a large hologram "STOP" sign blinks on and off every time the bus pulls to a curb.

This school bus also has an internal/external voice annunciation system which can deliver automatic messages on bus movements to pedestrians or programmed messages to passengers.

The engine is powered by compressed natural gas. School buses of the future will move down the highway on electric and other alternative fuel sources. At the present time, the high-efficiency diesel engines of newer school buses make the operation of these large machines an "environmental deal" when you consider each 50 passenger bus could eliminate 20 to 30 passenger cars on the road. The savings in fuel alone, make placing your children on a school bus a smart, environmental decision.

This concept bus leads to what has been called, "shared-use" vehicles. In many metropolitan communities transit buses ply the streets at the same time as yellow school buses are running their twice-daily routes.

Somewhere in our collective future we will have to resolve this duplication of services. In other words, is it possible to have one fleet of buses which would function as both a transit and school bus?

The financial pressures of tomorrow may dictate some reasoned planning on this issue today. You, as a parent, should insist on one prerequisite for any discussions on shared use:

the safety of your children will never be compromised.

And, with that statement, we conclude. This book was launched on the assumption that we live our lives by the numbers. Risk is only "reasonable" if the numbers are in our favor. We pull "one-armed bandits" in Las Vegas, insist on eating only low-fat potato chips and socking money away in a particular mutual fund—all based on the numbers.

Every school morning, this nation plays the numbers when almost 25 million children climb the metal stairwells of yellow school buses. And you know what, these numbers are exceptional, but not perfect.

The statistics are not perfect because, in a world where "human error" is always a possibility, there will be accidents and there will always be pain. There just is not enough money and intellect to build the "perfect" pupil transportation system. When trains, gravel trucks, and drunk drivers collide with a 30,000 pound school bus, there just is no system to protect everyone. But we can keep working on it.

I hope you will agree with me, the guy who, until three years ago, thought yellow school buses was a pain in the rear while trying to get home from the office—that each school day you want your child to be part of a miracle which will never make the 6 p.m. evening news.

When he/she safely walks through your front door, after traveling on a yellow school bus, you have just witnessed another **unreported miracle.**

BUSWORK

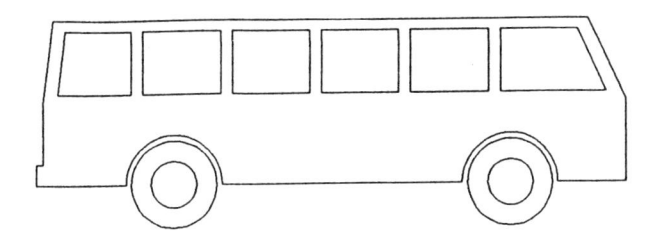

As a result of reading **Unreported Miracles**, here are some practical actions you can take to enhance the safety of your child(ren) as a passenger on a yellow school bus.

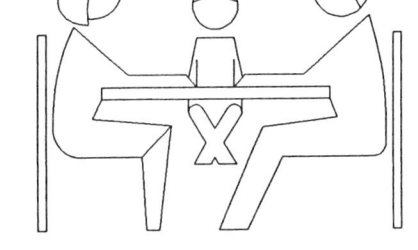

Before your child leaves for the bus stop. . .

conduct a "family meeting" to talk about the importance of your child's participation in school bus safety. In this session, address how important it is to get to the bus stop early, know the rules and respect the authority of the school bus driver.

Check your child's clothing. . .

bookbags, knapsacks and other pieces of "luggage" for any drawstrings which may become a safety hazard while boarding or deboarding a school bus. Also, constantly repeat the rule that in no circumstances should your child go back to retrieve an item after deboarding.

At least once, take your child to. . .

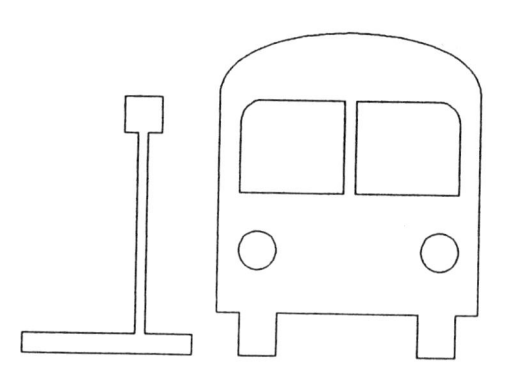

his/her school bus stop to observe, meet the driver, and remind your child to stand back at least 6 feet from the curb or edge of the road while waiting for the bus. You also may want to reverse this process by arriving when your child deboards the school bus.

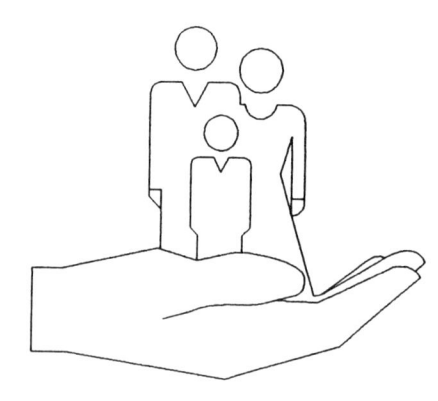

Get involved in your local. . .

parent-teacher association, school board meetings and other advocacy groups who share your interest in your child's safety. Pupil transportation is normally an important issue for these organizations.